BECOMING A MILLIONAIRE

Strategies of becoming a millionaire which are hidden from you.

Wayne Smith

Copyright © 2024 by Wayne Smith

All rights reserved.

No portion of this book may be reproduced in any form without written permission from the publisher or author, except as permitted by U.S. copyright law.

Table of contents

1. Introduction
    - Understanding the Millionaire Mindset
    - Setting Your Financial Goals
2. Financial Education
    - Importance of Financial Literacy
    - Learning about Investments
    - Understanding Risk and Reward
3. Earn More Money
    - Maximizing Your Income Potential
    - Exploring Entrepreneurship
    - Investing in Yourself: Education and Skills
4. Save and Invest Wisely
    - Budgeting Basics
    - Building an Emergency Fund
    - Investing Strategies for Long-Term Growth
5. Manage Debt Effectively
    - Strategies for Debt Reduction
    - Avoiding Bad Debt
    - Leveraging Debt for Wealth Building
6. Build Multiple Streams of Income
    - Diversifying Your Income Sources
    - Passive Income Opportunities
    - Creating Residual Income Streams

7. **Cultivate Discipline and Patience**
    - **Delayed Gratification: The Key to Success**
    - **Staying Focused on Long-Term Goals**
    - **Overcoming Challenges and Setbacks**
8. **Network and Surround Yourself with Success**
    - **Importance of Networking**
    - **Mentors and Role Models**
    - **Joining Mastermind Groups and Communities**
9. **Giving Back and Philanthropy**
    - **The Power of Giving**
    - **Incorporating Philanthropy into Your Financial Plan**
    - **Leaving a Legacy**
10. **Conclusion**
    - **Recap of Key Strategies**
    - **Taking Action on Your Path to Millionaire Success**

YOU THINK BECOMING A MILLIONAIRE TAKES A LOTS OF EXTRA SACRIFICE, THEN YOU LIE!

During his more than two decades as a CEO and serial entrepreneur, Wayne Smith has created five flagship companies across different industries, delivering tens of millions of dollar value to shareholders. In How to become a millionaire Smith defines the mindset that drives his remarkable success in corporate America.

Becoming a millionaire is different from any other book on the subject because Smith isn't selling investment tips, or motivational claptrap. He merely wants to help people embrace entrepreneurship, and to share lessons he learned the hard way.

Inside you'll learn

To understand the millionaire mindset and setting your financial goal.

The importance of financial literacy and learning about investments.

To save and invest in yourself through education and skills.

To build multiple streams of income and investing strategies for long-term growth and so many more.

Whether you're a laid-back dreamer or a busy bee looking to reduce your workload, this book is your ticket to financial freedom with a relaxed twist. Embrace the Smith millionaire mindset and start your journey to a richer, more leisure-filled life today!

Get your copy of Becoming a Millionaire and start your journey today!

INTRODUCTION

Understanding the Millionaire Mindset

In the pursuit of wealth and financial success, one of the most critical components is understanding the mindset that separates millionaires from the rest. Contrary to popular belief, becoming a millionaire is not merely about luck or inheritance; it requires a specific mindset, discipline, and strategic thinking. This chapter delves into the foundational principles of the millionaire mindset, exploring the attitudes, beliefs, and behaviors that pave the way to financial abundance.

The Power of Belief Systems:

At the core of the millionaire mindset lies a set of beliefs and attitudes that shape one's approach to money and success. These beliefs often develop early in life, influenced by family, culture, and personal experiences. While some individuals grow up with a scarcity mindset, believing that opportunities are limited and wealth is elusive, millionaires embrace an abundance mentality. They believe in their ability to createEmbracing Risk and Opportunity:

Another hallmark of the millionaire mindset is a willingness to embrace risk and seize opportunities. While many people shy away from uncertainty and prefer the safety of the familiar, millionaires understand that calculated risks are essential for growth and innovation. They carefully assess potential opportunities, weighing the potential rewards against the risks involved, and are not afraid to step outside their comfort zones in pursuit of greater success.

Continuous Learning and Adaptation:

Millionaires recognize that success is not a destination but a journey, requiring continuous learning and adaptation. They invest in their personal and professional development, seeking out opportunities to expand their knowledge and skills. Whether through formal education, mentorship, or self-directed learning, they are committed to staying ahead of the curve and adapting to changing market conditions.

Persistence and Resilience:

Perhaps the most crucial aspect of the millionaire mindset is persistence and resilience in the face of challenges. Building wealth is rarely a linear path, and setbacks are inevitable along the way. However, millionaires do not let failure deter them; instead, they view it as a valuable learning experience and an opportunity for growth. With unwavering determination and a positive attitude, they persevere through adversity and ultimately emerge stronger and more resilient.

wealth, viewing obstacles as temporary challenges rather than insurmountable barriers.

Setting Your Financial Goals

Goal Setting and Visualization:

Millionaires understand the importance of setting clear, achievable goals and visualizing their success. By envisioning their desired outcomes with vivid detail, they create a roadmap for achievement and stay motivated even in the face of adversity. Visualization techniques, such as creating vision boards or practicing daily affirmations, help reinforce their commitment to their goals and align their actions with their aspirationsFocus on Long-Term Wealth Building:

While some individuals may seek quick fixes or instant gratification, millionaires understand the importance of long-term wealth building. They prioritize strategic planning and disciplined saving and investing over short-term gains. By focusing on building sustainable wealth that can withstand economic fluctuations, they create a solid financial foundation for themselves and future generations.

Mindful Spending and Living Below Means:

Contrary to the stereotype of extravagant spending, many millionaires practice mindful spending and live below their means. They prioritize value over status symbols and avoid unnecessary expenses that detract from their long-term financial goals. By adopting a frugal mindset and making conscious choices about how they allocate their resources, they maximize their wealth-building potential and create lasting prosperity.

Giving Back and Leaving a Legacy:

Finally, millionaires understand the importance of giving back to their communities and leaving a legacy of impact. They recognize that true wealth is not just measured in monetary terms but also in the positive influence they have on others. Whether through philanthropy, mentorship, or civic engagement, they use their resources and influence to make a difference in the world and create a lasting legacy that extends far beyond their financial success.

Conclusion:

In conclusion, the millionaire mindset is a multifaceted approach to wealth creation that encompasses beliefs, attitudes, and behaviors conducive to financial success. By adopting the principles outlined in this chapter—developing a positive relationship with money, building self-confidence, embracing entrepreneurship, focusing on long-term wealth building, mindful spending, and giving back—you can begin to cultivate your own millionaire mindset and pave the way to financial abundance. In the chapters that follow, we will delve deeper into practical strategies and techniques for implementing these principles and achieving your millionaire goals.

Financial Education

Importance of Financial Literacy

Financial literacy is the cornerstone of financial success. In today's complex and ever-changing world, understanding how money works is essential for making informed decisions, managing personal finances, and building wealth. This chapter explores the importance of financial literacy, highlighting its impact on individual and societal well-being, and providing insights into how improving financial literacy can empower individuals to achieve their financial goals.

Understanding the Basics:

At its core, financial literacy refers to the knowledge and skills needed to make sound financial decisions. This includes understanding fundamental concepts such as budgeting, saving, investing, debt management, and risk management. Without a solid grasp of these basics, individuals may struggle to navigate the complexities of modern financial systems and may be more susceptible to financial pitfalls and scams.

Empowerment Through Education:

Financial literacy empowers individuals to take control of their financial futures. By arming themselves with knowledge, individuals can make informed decisions that align with their goals and values. Whether it's saving for retirement, buying a home, or starting a business, financial literacy provides the tools and confidence needed to navigate life's financial challenges with ease.

Breaking the Cycle of Poverty:

Financial literacy plays a crucial role in breaking the cycle of poverty and promoting economic mobility. Individuals who lack basic financial knowledge may find themselves trapped in a cycle of debt and financial insecurity, with limited opportunities for upward mobility. By providing access to financial education and resources, communities can empower individuals to build brighter futures for themselves and their families.

Building Wealth and Financial Security:

Financial literacy is the foundation of wealth building and financial security. Individuals who understand how to manage their money effectively are better positioned to grow their wealth over time through saving and investing. They are also more adept at protecting their assets and mitigating risks, ensuring long-term financial stability for themselves and their loved ones.

Making Informed Decisions:

In today's complex financial landscape, individuals are faced with a myriad of financial products and services, each with its own risks and benefits. Without a basic understanding of financial concepts, individuals may struggle to evaluate these options and make informed decisions. Financial literacy equips individuals with the critical thinking skills needed to assess financial products, identify potential risks, and choose the options that best align with their needs and goals.

Protecting Against Financial Exploitation:

Financial literacy also serves as a defense against financial exploitation and fraud. Individuals who are well-informed about common scams and fraudulent practices are less likely to fall victim to them. By recognizing warning signs and knowing how to protect themselves, individuals can safeguard their finances and avoid devastating losses.

Promoting Financial Well-Being:

Beyond the practical benefits, financial literacy is also closely linked to overall well-being and quality of life. Individuals who feel confident in their financial knowledge and skills are less likely to experience stress and anxiety related to money. They are also more likely to enjoy greater financial independence and freedom, allowing them to pursue their passions and live life on their own terms.

Learning about Investments

Investing is a powerful tool for building wealth and achieving financial independence. However, many people are intimidated by the world of investments, feeling overwhelmed by the complexity of financial markets and unsure where to begin. This chapter aims to demystify the process of investing, providing readers with a comprehensive overview of different investment options, strategies, and considerations.

Understanding Investment Basics:

Before diving into specific investment opportunities, it's essential to understand the fundamental principles of investing. At its core, investing involves putting money into assets with the expectation of generating returns over time. These assets can include stocks, bonds, real estate, commodities, and more. By allocating capital strategically, investors aim to grow their wealth and achieve their financial goals.

Types of Investments:

Investments come in various shapes and sizes, each with its own risk and return characteristics. Some common types of investments include:

1. Stocks: Ownership shares in a company, offering potential for capital appreciation and dividends.
2. Bonds: Debt securities issued by governments or corporations, providing regular interest payments and return of principal at maturity.
3. Real Estate: Ownership of physical property or real estate investment trusts (REITs), offering rental income and potential for property appreciation.
4. Mutual Funds: Pooled investment vehicles that invest in a diversified portfolio of stocks, bonds, or other assets, managed by professional fund managers.
5. Exchange-Traded Funds (ETFs): Similar to mutual funds but traded on stock exchanges, offering diversification and liquidity.
6. Commodities: Physical goods such as gold, oil, and agricultural products, offering

diversification and potential protection against inflation.

Risk and Return:

One of the fundamental principles of investing is the trade-off between risk and return. Generally, investments with higher potential returns also come with higher levels of risk. Understanding your risk tolerance and investment objectives is essential for building a well-balanced investment portfolio that aligns with your financial goals. Diversification, or spreading investments across different asset classes, can help mitigate risk and enhance long-term returns.

Investment Strategies:

There are various investment strategies that investors can employ to achieve their financial objectives. Some common strategies include:

1. Buy and Hold: Investing in quality assets with a long-term perspective, aiming to ride out market fluctuations and capture the benefits of compounding over time.
2. Value Investing: Identifying undervalued assets with the potential for long-term growth, based on fundamental analysis of financial metrics and market conditions.

3. Growth Investing: Investing in companies with strong growth potential, focusing on factors such as revenue growth, market share, and innovation.
4. Income Investing: Seeking investments that generate regular income, such as dividend-paying stocks, bonds, or real estate investment trusts (REITs).
5. Asset Allocation: Allocating investment capital across different asset classes based on risk tolerance, time horizon, and investment objectives, aiming to optimize risk-adjusted returns.
6. Dollar-Cost Averaging: Investing a fixed amount of money at regular intervals, regardless of market conditions, to reduce the impact of market volatility on investment returns.

Due Diligence and Research:

Before making any investment decisions, it's essential to conduct thorough due diligence and research. This includes analyzing financial statements, assessing market trends, and evaluating the track record of investment managers. It's also crucial to consider factors such as fees, taxes, and liquidity when selecting investment vehicles. By taking the time to research and understand potential investments, investors can make more informed decisions and avoid costly mistakes.

Understanding Risk and Reward

Risk and reward are two fundamental concepts in the world of finance and investing. Every investment decision involves a trade-off between these two factors: the potential for higher returns comes with the possibility of greater risk. In this chapter, we will explore the relationship between risk and reward, examine different types of risk investors face, and discuss strategies for managing risk while maximizing potential rewards.

Defining Risk and Reward:

Risk refers to the uncertainty or variability of returns associated with an investment. It encompasses the possibility of losing some or all of the invested capital, as well as the potential for returns to deviate from expected outcomes. Reward, on the other hand, represents the potential gains or returns investors can earn from their investments. It is the compensation investors receive for taking on risk.

Types of Risk:

There are several types of risk that investors may encounter when investing:

1. Market Risk: Also known as systematic risk, market risk refers to the risk of losses due to factors that affect the overall performance of the financial markets, such as economic downturns, geopolitical events, or changes in interest rates.
2. Company-Specific Risk: Also known as unsystematic risk, company-specific risk refers to the risk of losses associated with individual companies or assets. This may include factors such as poor management, competitive pressures, or regulatory changes that affect specific companies or industries.
3. Credit Risk: Credit risk refers to the risk of losses due to the failure of a borrower to repay a loan or debt obligation. It is commonly associated with bonds or fixed-income securities issued by governments or corporations.
4. Liquidity Risk: Liquidity risk refers to the risk of being unable to buy or sell an investment quickly and at a fair price. Investments with low liquidity may be more susceptible to

price fluctuations and may incur higher transaction costs.
5. Inflation Risk: Inflation risk refers to the risk that the purchasing power of an investment will be eroded over time due to inflation. Investments that fail to keep pace with inflation may experience a decline in real value over time.
6. Currency Risk: Currency risk refers to the risk of losses due to fluctuations in foreign exchange rates. Investors who hold assets denominated in foreign currencies may experience losses if the value of the currency depreciates relative to their own currency.

The Risk-Return Tradeoff:

The risk-return tradeoff is a fundamental principle in finance that states that higher levels of risk are generally associated with higher potential returns, and vice versa. This relationship forms the basis of investment decision-making, as investors must weigh the potential rewards of an investment against the risks involved.Strategies for Managing Risk:

While it is impossible to eliminate risk entirely, investors can take steps to manage and mitigate risk in their investment portfolios:

1. Diversification: Diversification involves spreading investment capital across different asset classes, sectors, and geographic regions to reduce the impact of any single investment or event on the overall portfolio. By diversifying, investors can minimize company-specific risk and improve the risk-return profile of their portfolios.
2. Asset Allocation: Asset allocation involves determining the mix of asset classes (such as stocks, bonds, and cash) that best aligns with an investor's risk tolerance, time horizon, and investment objectives. By allocating investment capital strategically, investors can balance risk and return and optimize the performance of their portfolios.
3. Risk Management Strategies: Risk management strategies, such as setting stop-loss orders, implementing hedging strategies, or using derivatives, can help investors mitigate specific risks in their portfolios. These strategies are particularly useful for managing downside risk and protecting against large losses.
4. Regular Review and Rebalancing: Regularly reviewing and rebalancing investment portfolios is essential for maintaining the desired risk-return profile over time. This

may involve selling investments that have become overvalued or overweighted and reallocating capital to investments that offer better risk-adjusted returns.

Conclusion:

Risk and reward are inherent aspects of investing, and understanding the relationship between them is crucial for making informed investment decisions. By recognizing the types of risk investors face, understanding the risk-return tradeoff, and implementing strategies for managing risk, investors can build well-balanced investment portfolios that align with their financial goals and risk tolerance.

Earn More Money

Maximizing Your Income Potential

In today's dynamic and competitive economy, maximizing your income potential is essential for achieving financial security and building wealth. Whether you're aiming to increase your salary, start a side hustle, or invest in your education and skills, there are numerous strategies you can employ to boost your earning power. This comprehensive guide will explore various avenues for maximizing your income potential, providing practical tips and insights to help you take control of your financial future.

1. Enhancing Your Skills and Education:

Investing in your education and skill development is one of the most effective ways to increase your income potential. Whether through formal education, vocational training, or online courses, acquiring new skills and qualifications can open doors to higher-paying job opportunities and career advancement. Consider pursuing certifications or advanced degrees in fields that are in high demand, or developing expertise in emerging industries such as technology, healthcare, or finance.

2. **Negotiating Your Salary:**

Negotiating your salary is a crucial step in maximizing your income potential, yet many people shy away from this conversation. Researching industry salary benchmarks, highlighting your accomplishments and contributions, and confidently articulating your value to employers can significantly increase your earning potential. Don't be afraid to advocate for yourself and negotiate for the compensation you deserve.

3. **Pursuing Career Advancement Opportunities:**

Advancing in your career can lead to higher earning potential and greater job satisfaction. Take initiative in seeking out opportunities for promotion or advancement within your current organization, such as taking on leadership roles, spearheading projects, or seeking additional responsibilities. Alternatively, consider exploring opportunities for career growth and advancement outside of your current company, such as networking, attending industry events, or leveraging online platforms like LinkedIn to connect with potential employers.

4. **Starting a Side Hustle:**

Starting a side hustle can be a lucrative way to supplement your income and diversify your revenue streams. Whether it's freelancing, consulting, selling products online, or starting a small business, there are countless opportunities to monetize your skills and interests. Identify your strengths and passions, research market demand, and develop a viable business plan to launch your side hustle successfully. With dedication and perseverance, your side hustle has the potential to grow into a full-fledged business and become a significant source of income.

5. **Investing in Real Estate:**

Real estate investing is another avenue for maximizing your income potential and building long-term wealth. Whether through rental properties, real estate investment trusts (REITs), or property flipping, real estate offers opportunities for passive income, capital appreciation, and tax benefits. Conduct thorough market research, assess your risk tolerance, and explore different investment strategies to determine the best approach for your financial goals.

6. **Leveraging the Gig Economy:**

The rise of the gig economy has created new opportunities for earning income on a flexible, freelance basis. Platforms like Uber, Lyft, TaskRabbit, and Upwork offer opportunities to earn money on your own schedule, whether through driving, delivery, freelance work, or odd jobs. While gig work may not offer the stability of traditional employment, it can provide valuable supplemental income and flexibility to balance work with other commitments.

7. **Investing in Stocks and Financial Markets**:

Investing in stocks and financial markets is a time-tested strategy for growing wealth and maximizing income potential. Whether through individual stocks, mutual funds, exchange-traded funds (ETFs), or retirement accounts, investing in the stock market offers the potential for capital appreciation and dividend income over time. Conduct thorough research, diversify your portfolio, and consult with a financial advisor to develop an investment strategy that aligns with your risk tolerance and financial goals.

8. **Monetizing Your Passion:**

Monetizing your passion is not only a fulfilling way to earn income but can also be highly profitable. Whether it's writing, photography, cooking, crafting, or any other hobby or skill, there are numerous opportunities to turn your passion into a source of income. Consider monetizing your expertise through teaching, coaching, creating digital products, or launching a blog or YouTube channel. With creativity and perseverance, you can turn your passion into a profitable venture that generates income for years to come.

9. **Maximizing Your Savings and Investments:**

Maximizing your income potential isn't just about earning more money; it's also about managing and growing your wealth effectively. Make it a priority to save and invest a portion of your income regularly, taking advantage of tax-advantaged accounts such as 401(k)s, IRAs, and HSAs. Automate your savings and investment contributions to ensure consistency, and explore opportunities to optimize your investment returns through strategies such as dollar-cost averaging, asset allocation, and tax-efficient investing.

10. **Continuing to Learn and Adapt:**

Finally, maximizing your income potential requires a commitment to lifelong learning and adaptation. Stay informed about industry trends, technological advancements, and market developments that may impact your earning potential. Continuously seek out opportunities to expand your skills, network with other professionals, and stay ahead of the curve in your field. By remaining proactive and adaptable, you can position yourself for ongoing success and maximize your income potential in the long term.

Exploring Entrepreneurship

Entrepreneurship represents a journey of innovation, creativity, and ambition. It's the pursuit of turning ideas into reality, creating value, and making a positive impact on the world. In this comprehensive guide, we'll delve into the world of entrepreneurship, exploring the opportunities it presents, the challenges it entails, and the strategies for success.Entrepreneurship is more than just starting a business; it's a mindset, a way of thinking and approaching the world. At its core, entrepreneurship involves identifying opportunities, taking calculated risks, and pursuing innovative solutions to solve problems or meet unmet needs. Whether you're launching a tech startup, a small business, or a social enterprise, entrepreneurship requires vision, determination, and resilience.One of the first steps in exploring entrepreneurship is identifying opportunities for innovation and value creation. This may involve spotting gaps in the market, identifying emerging trends, or solving problems that others have overlooked. By observing the world around you, listening to customers, and staying curious, you can uncover opportunities that have the potential to become successful ventures.Entrepreneurship is not without its challenges. From securing funding and building a team to navigating regulatory hurdles and managing cash flow, entrepreneurs face a myriad of obstacles on the road to success. However, with perseverance, resourcefulness, and a willingness to learn from failure, many entrepreneurs are able to overcome these challenges and emerge stronger and more resilient.A well-thought-out business plan is essential for guiding your entrepreneurial journey and securing support from investors, lenders, and stakeholders. Your business plan should outline your vision, mission, target market, competitive landscape, marketing strategy, financial projections, and operational plan. It serves as a roadmap for your business, helping you stay focused on your goals and navigate the complexities of entrepreneurship.

Building a strong team is essential for the success of any entrepreneurial venture. Surrounding yourself with talented, passionate individuals who share your vision and complement your skills can help propel your business forward and overcome obstacles along the way. Whether you're recruiting employees, co-founders, or advisors, prioritize hiring individuals who are aligned with your values and committed to the success of the business. Building a strong brand and customer base is essential for the long-term success of any business. By delivering exceptional products or services, providing outstanding customer service, and cultivating a loyal customer following, entrepreneurs can differentiate themselves from competitors and build a sustainable business that stands the test of time. Invest in building relationships with your customers, soliciting feedback, and continually refining your offerings to meet their needs and preferences.

Finally, entrepreneurship is a journey of highs and lows, successes and setbacks. Celebrate your successes, no matter how small, and use them as fuel to propel you forward. At the same time, embrace failure as an opportunity for growth and learning. Analyze what went wrong, identify lessons learned, and use them to inform your future decisions and actions. Remember that failure is not the end of the road but rather a stepping stone on the path to success.Exploring entrepreneurship is a rewarding and transformative journey that offers endless opportunities for innovation, growth, and impact. Whether you're a seasoned entrepreneur or just starting out, the key to success lies in vision, determination, and a willingness to embrace challenges and opportunities along the way. By understanding the fundamentals of entrepreneurship, identifying opportunities, navigating challenges, and building a strong foundation for your business, you can unlock your full potential as an entrepreneur and create a lasting legacy in the world.

Investing in Yourself: Education and Skills
Investing in yourself is one of the most valuable investments you can make. By continuously improving your skills, expanding your knowledge, and honing your abilities, you not only enhance your personal and professional development but also increase your earning potential and open doors to new opportunities. In this comprehensive guide, we'll explore the importance of investing in yourself through education and skills development, and provide practical strategies for maximizing the returns on this investment.

Education and skills development are the foundation of personal and professional growth. Whether through formal education, vocational training, or self-directed learning, investing in your education and skills enables you to acquire new knowledge, gain valuable expertise, and enhance your capabilities. In today's rapidly evolving job market, continuous learning is essential for staying competitive and adapting to changing industry trends and technological advancements.

Before embarking on your journey of self-improvement, it's important to identify your learning objectives and goals. What skills do you want to develop? What knowledge do you want to acquire? By clarifying your objectives, you can focus your

efforts on areas that align with your interests, strengths, and career aspirations. Whether you're seeking to advance in your current role, transition to a new career, or pursue personal interests, having clear goals will guide your learning journey.
Formal education, such as attending college, university, or vocational school, remains a valuable investment in yourself. Whether pursuing a degree, certification, or specialized training program, formal education provides structured learning opportunities, access to expert instructors, and credentials that can enhance your credibility and marketability in the job market. Consider exploring programs that offer flexible schedules, online learning options, and financial aid opportunities to accommodate your needs and budget.Investing in yourself is not a one-time event but a lifelong journey of continuous improvement and growth. Make learning a habit by dedicating time each day or week to engage in activities that expand your knowledge and skills. Whether it's reading books, listening to podcasts, watching instructional videos, or experimenting with new techniques, commit to lifelong learning and embrace opportunities for growth and development in all aspects of your life. Investing in yourself through education and skills development is one of the most valuable investments you can make. By continuously

expanding your knowledge, honing your abilities, and embracing opportunities for growth and development, you position yourself for success in your personal and professional life. Whether through formal education, online learning.

Save and Invest Wisely

Budgeting Basics
Budgeting is the process of creating a plan for how you will allocate your income to meet your expenses and financial goals. It provides clarity and insight into your financial situation, allowing you to make informed decisions about spending, saving, and investing. By creating a budget, you can identify areas where you may be overspending, prioritize your financial goals, and take proactive steps to achieve them.

To create a budget, start by gathering information about your income, expenses, and financial goals. Your income includes sources such as salary, wages, bonuses, and any other sources of income. Your expenses include fixed expenses such as rent, mortgage, utilities, and loan payments, as well as variable expenses such as groceries, transportation, entertainment, and discretionary spending.

Once you have a clear understanding of your income and expenses, categorize your expenses into essential and non-essential categories. Essential expenses are those that are necessary for basic living needs, such as housing, food, and transportation, while non-essential expenses are those that are optional or discretionary, such as dining out, entertainment, and luxury purchases. Setting financial goals is an essential part of the budgeting process. Your financial goals may include paying off debt, saving for emergencies, buying a home, funding your retirement, or achieving other long-term objectives. By setting specific, measurable, achievable, relevant, and time-bound (SMART) goals, you can create a roadmap for your financial future and stay motivated to stick to your budget.One of the most important components of a solid financial plan is building an emergency fund. An emergency fund is a savings account that is specifically earmarked for unexpected expenses or financial emergencies, such as medical bills, car repairs, or job loss. Aim to save enough to cover three to six months' worth of living expenses in your emergency fund to provide a financial safety net and peace of mind in times of need.

Budgeting is a powerful tool that empowers individuals to take control of their finances, achieve their goals, and build a solid foundation for financial well-being. By understanding the importance of budgeting, setting financial goals, tracking your spending, making adjustments as needed, building an emergency fund, avoiding debt, and seeking professional guidance when needed, you can create a budget that aligns with your priorities and helps you achieve financial success. Remember that budgeting is a journey, not a destination, and that consistency and discipline are key to long-term financial health.

Building an Emergency Fund

An emergency fund is a crucial component of financial stability and preparedness. It acts as a safety net, providing a buffer against unexpected expenses, financial setbacks, and life's uncertainties. In this comprehensive guide, we'll explore the importance of building an emergency fund, strategies for saving, and tips for managing and maximizing your emergency fund.

Life is unpredictable, and unexpected expenses can arise at any time. From medical emergencies and car repairs to job loss and natural disasters, having an emergency fund can provide peace of mind and financial security in times of need. An emergency fund allows you to cover unexpected expenses without resorting to high-interest debt, liquidating investments, or relying on assistance from family and friends.

The first step in building an emergency fund is setting a savings goal. Financial experts generally recommend saving enough to cover three to six months' worth of living expenses in your emergency fund. This provides a sufficient financial cushion to cover unexpected expenses and maintain your standard of living in the event of a job loss or other financial hardship. However, your ideal savings goal may vary depending on factors such as your income, expenses, job stability, and risk tolerance. Once you've established your emergency fund goal, create a budget to save. Start by identifying areas where you can reduce discretionary spending and reallocate funds toward savings. Cut back on non-essential expenses such as dining out, entertainment, and luxury purchases, and redirect those funds to your emergency fund. Consider automating your savings by setting up automatic transfers from your checking account to your emergency fund each month.

Building an emergency fund requires discipline and commitment, especially in the face of temptation to spend impulsively or deviate from your savings plan. Avoid the temptation to dip into your emergency fund for non-essential expenses or purchases. Remember that your emergency fund is for emergencies only and should be reserved for unexpected expenses that threaten your financial stability. Stay focused on your long-term financial goals and resist the urge to sabotage your progress with unnecessary spending.

Building an emergency fund is a critical step in achieving financial stability and peace of mind. By setting a savings goal, creating a budget, choosing the right savings vehicle, making regular contributions, utilizing windfalls and bonuses, avoiding temptation, reviewing and adjusting your plan, and managing your emergency fund effectively, you can build a solid financial safety net that protects you against unexpected expenses and financial hardships. Remember that building an emergency fund is a journey, not a destination, and that consistency and discipline are key to long-term success. Start saving today and take control of your financial future.

Investing Strategies for Long-Term Growth
Investing for long-term growth is a key strategy for building wealth, achieving financial independence, and securing your financial future. While short-term fluctuations in the market are inevitable, adopting a long-term investment approach allows you to

capitalize on the power of compounding and ride out market volatility. In this guide, we'll explore various investment strategies for long-term growth, including diversification, asset allocation, dollar-cost averaging, and the importance of staying disciplined and patient.

Diversification is a fundamental investment strategy for managing risk and maximizing returns over the long term. By spreading your investment capital across different asset classes, sectors, and geographic regions, you can reduce the impact of any single investment or event on your overall portfolio. Diversification helps to mitigate risk and increase the likelihood of achieving consistent returns over time, regardless of market conditions.

Investing in quality companies with strong fundamentals and competitive advantages is another key strategy for long-term growth. Look for companies with solid financials, consistent earnings growth, a strong market position, and a track record of innovation and adaptability. Focus on companies with sustainable competitive advantages, such as brand loyalty, economies of scale, or proprietary technology, that are well-positioned to thrive in the long term.

One of the most important aspects of successful long-term investing is staying disciplined and patient, especially during periods of market volatility or economic uncertainty. Avoid succumbing to short-term market fluctuations or trying to time the market, as this can lead to emotional decision-making and undermine your long-term investment goals. Instead, focus on your investment strategy, stick to your asset allocation plan, and remain committed to your long-term financial objectives.

Investing for long-term growth is a proven strategy for building wealth and achieving financial independence over time. By diversifying your portfolio, allocating assets strategically, employing dollar-cost averaging, investing in quality companies, considering growth versus value stocks, reinvesting dividends, and staying disciplined and patient, you can maximize your investment returns and achieve your long-term financial goals. Remember that successful long-term investing requires a commitment to consistency, discipline, and a focus on the big picture. Start investing for the long term today and set yourself on the path to financial success.

Manage Debt Effectively

Strategies for Debt Reduction

Debt can be a significant burden on your finances, causing stress, limiting your financial freedom, and hindering your ability to achieve your goals. Fortunately, there are strategies you can employ to reduce and ultimately eliminate your debt. In this guide, we'll explore various debt reduction strategies, from prioritizing high-interest debt to budgeting effectively and seeking professional assistance when needed.

When it comes to debt reduction, it's essential to prioritize high-interest debt, such as credit card debt, personal loans, or payday loans. High-interest debt can quickly spiral out of control due to compounding interest, making it challenging to pay off over time. Start by focusing on paying off your highest-interest debt first, while making minimum payments on other debts. Once you've paid off your high-interest debt, you can allocate more funds toward paying off lower-interest debt.

Budgeting is a critical component of debt reduction, as it allows you to track your income and expenses, identify areas where you can cut back, and allocate more funds toward debt repayment. Create a monthly budget that outlines your income, fixed expenses (such as rent or mortgage, utilities, and loan payments), variable expenses (such as groceries, transportation, and entertainment), and debt payments. Look for opportunities to reduce discretionary spending and redirect those funds toward debt repayment.If you're struggling to make payments on your debts, consider reaching out to your creditors to negotiate more favorable terms. Many creditors are willing to work with borrowers who are experiencing financial hardship, offering options such as reduced interest rates, extended repayment terms, or debt settlement agreements. Be honest and transparent about your financial situation, and be prepared to provide documentation to support your request for assistance.

While you're working toward paying off existing debt, it's essential to avoid taking on new debt whenever possible. This means resisting the temptation to use credit cards for discretionary purchases, taking out new loans, or financing purchases with high-interest payment plans. Instead, focus on living within your means, sticking to your budget, and prioritizing debt repayment until you've achieved your financial goals.

Reducing and ultimately eliminating debt is an achievable goal with the right strategies and mindset. By prioritizing high-interest debt, creating a debt repayment plan, budgeting effectively, considering debt consolidation, negotiating with creditors, increasing your income, avoiding new debt, and seeking professional assistance if needed, you can take control of your finances and achieve financial freedom. Remember that debt reduction is a journey, and progress may take time, but with determination and perseverance, you can overcome debt and build a brighter financial future for yourself.

Avoiding Bad Debt

Debt can be a double-edged sword. When managed responsibly, it can facilitate important investments and provide financial flexibility. However, not all debt is created equal. Bad debt, characterized by high interest rates, unnecessary spending, and financial strain, can quickly derail your financial well-being.

Bad debt refers to borrowing money for non-essential purchases or expenses that do not contribute to your long-term financial well-being. It typically carries high-interest rates, making it expensive to repay over time. Examples of bad debt include credit card debt used for luxury purchases, payday loans with exorbitant interest rates, and auto loans for vehicles beyond your means. Bad debt can quickly accumulate, leading to financial stress, limited savings, and difficulty achieving your financial goals.

The consequences of bad debt can be far-reaching and detrimental to your financial health. High-interest debt can quickly spiral out of control, leading to a cycle of borrowing and repayment that drains your resources and limits your financial freedom. Bad debt can also negatively impact your credit score, making it more difficult to qualify for loans, obtain favorable interest rates, or secure housing and employment opportunities.

Additionally, the stress and anxiety associated with bad debt can take a toll on your mental and emotional well-being, affecting your overall quality of life.

One of the most effective ways to avoid bad debt is to live within your means. This means spending less than you earn and prioritizing needs over wants. Create a realistic budget that accounts for your income, expenses, and financial goals, and stick to it. Avoid the temptation to overspend on non-essential purchases or luxuries that you cannot afford.

Building an emergency fund is essential for protecting yourself against unexpected expenses and financial emergencies. By setting aside a portion of your income in a savings account, you can avoid having to rely on high-interest debt to cover unforeseen costs. Aim to save enough to cover three to six months' worth of living expenses in your emergency fund to provide a financial safety net.

If you do have existing debt, prioritize paying off high-interest debt first. This may include credit card debt, payday loans, or other forms of high-interest borrowing. By focusing on paying off high-interest debt first, you can save money on interest payments and accelerate your progress toward debt-free living.

Finally, seek out financial education and assistance to help you make informed decisions about your finances and avoid bad debt. Take advantage of resources such as financial literacy courses, workshops, and online resources to improve your financial knowledge and skills. If you're struggling with debt, don't hesitate to seek professional assistance from a credit counselor or financial advisor who can provide personalized guidance and support.

Avoiding bad debt is essential for building financial health and achieving your long-term financial goals. By living within your means, building an emergency fund, using credit wisely, avoiding payday loans and cash advances, prioritizing high-interest debt, being wary of impulse purchases, and seeking financial education and assistance, you can protect yourself against the negative consequences of bad debt and pave the way for a brighter financial future. Remember that avoiding bad debt requires discipline, awareness, and a commitment to making smart financial choices.

Leveraging Debt for Wealth Building

Debt is often viewed in a negative light, associated with financial stress and burden. However, when used strategically, debt can be a powerful tool for building wealth and achieving financial prosperity. Leveraging debt involves borrowing money to invest in assets or opportunities that have the potential to generate a return greater than the cost of borrowing.

Leveraged investing involves using borrowed funds to increase the size of your investment position, thereby amplifying potential returns. When you invest with borrowed money, you have the opportunity to benefit from the growth of your investments without having to use all of your own capital. This can magnify returns when investments perform well, leading to accelerated wealth accumulation. When leveraging debt for wealth building, focus on investments that generate income or have the potential for appreciation. Income-producing assets such as rental properties, dividend-paying stocks, and interest-bearing bonds can help offset the cost of borrowing and provide a steady stream of cash flow.When using margin trading or other forms of leverage, it's important to maintain a margin of safety to protect against potential losses. Avoid borrowing more than you can afford to repay, and have a plan in place to manage downside risk.

Leveraged investing is best suited for long-term investors with a time horizon of five years or more. Focus on investments with strong growth potential and the ability to withstand market fluctuations over the long term.Keep a close eye on your leveraged investments and regularly monitor their performance. Be prepared to adjust your strategy if market conditions change or if your investments are not performing as expected.

Leveraging debt for wealth building can be a powerful strategy for accelerating wealth accumulation and achieving financial prosperity. By strategically borrowing to invest in income-producing assets, diversifying your investments, maintaining a margin of safety, focusing on long-term growth, and monitoring your investments closely, you can leverage debt effectively to build wealth over time. However, it's important to carefully consider the risks involved and to approach leveraged investing with caution and discipline. With prudent planning and careful execution, leveraging debt can be a valuable tool for achieving your financial goals and securing your financial future.

Build Multiple Streams of Income

Diversifying Your Income Sources

In today's rapidly changing economy, relying solely on a single source of income can leave you vulnerable to financial instability. Diversifying your income sources is a proactive strategy for building resilience, reducing risk, and achieving greater financial stability.

Income diversification involves generating revenue from multiple sources, rather than relying solely on a single source of income such as a salary from a traditional job. Diversification spreads risk across different income streams, helping to mitigate the impact of economic downturns, industry disruptions, or unexpected life events. By diversifying your income sources, you can create a more robust financial foundation and increase your ability to weather financial challenges.

Diversifying your income reduces dependence on any single source of revenue, making you less vulnerable to disruptions in the economy or changes in the job market. If one income stream experiences a downturn, others may continue to generate revenue, helping to offset losses and maintain financial stability. Diversifying your income can open up opportunities for additional revenue streams and income growth. By exploring different sources of income, you can identify new ways to leverage your skills, expertise, and resources to increase your earning potential and achieve greater financial success.You may have the flexibility to pursue entrepreneurial ventures, freelance opportunities, or passion projects that align with your interests and goals. Multiple income streams can also provide greater autonomy and control over your financial future.

Launching a side business or entrepreneurial venture is one of the most common ways to diversify your income. Identify your skills, interests, and passions, and explore opportunities to monetize them. Whether it's starting an online store, offering freelance services, or launching a consulting business, a side business can provide an additional source of income and potential for growth.: If you have knowledge in a particular area, consider creating and monetizing content through platforms such as YouTube, podcasts, blogs, or online courses. Content creation allows you to leverage your expertise to reach a wide audience and generate revenue through advertising, sponsorships, subscriptions, or product sales. Explore opportunities to monetize your hobbies and interests by turning them into income-generating activities. Whether it's photography, crafting, cooking, or fitness, there may be opportunities to monetize your passions through teaching, selling products or services, or hosting events or workshops.

Diversifying your income sources is a powerful strategy for building financial resilience, stability, and prosperity. By generating revenue from multiple sources, you can reduce risk, increase stability, and unlock new opportunities for growth and income. Whether it's starting a side business, investing in real estate, creating and monetizing content, freelancing or consulting, or exploring other income-generating activities, there are countless ways to diversify your income and achieve greater financial well-being. Take proactive steps to diversify your income today and set yourself on the path to financial success and freedom.

Passive Income Opportunities

Passive income offers a pathway to financial freedom and flexibility by allowing you to generate revenue with minimal ongoing effort or active involvement. Unlike traditional forms of income, which require trading time for money, passive income streams can provide a steady stream of cash flow, allowing you to build wealth and achieve your financial goals.

Passive income is income that you earn with little to no ongoing effort or active involvement. It is generated from assets or investments that produce cash flow without requiring constant attention or hands-on management. Passive income streams can come from a variety of sources, including rental properties, dividend-paying stocks, interest-bearing investments, royalties, licensing agreements, and online businesses. The key characteristic of passive income is that it continues to generate revenue even when you're not actively working.It provides financial freedom by allowing you to generate income without being tied to a traditional job or trading time for money. It gives you the flexibility to pursue your interests, spend time with loved ones, and live life on your own terms.Passive income allows you to earn money while freeing up time for other pursuits, such as traveling, hobbies, or spending time with family and friends. It provides a source of income that is not directly tied to the number of hours worked, giving you more control over your time and priorities.

Building an online business or passive income stream can provide opportunities to earn money with minimal ongoing effort. This includes creating and selling digital products, such as e-books, courses, templates, or software, or monetizing a website or blog through advertising, affiliate marketing, or sponsored content.If you have creative works or intellectual property, you can earn passive income through royalties and licensing agreements. This includes income from books, music, artwork, patents, trademarks, and software. By licensing your intellectual property to third parties, you can earn royalties based on sales or usage.

Passive income offers a powerful pathway to financial freedom, allowing you to generate income with minimal ongoing effort or active involvement. By diversifying your income with passive streams, you can build resilience, stability, and wealth over time. Whether it's through rental properties, dividend-paying stocks, interest-bearing investments, royalties, online businesses, peer-to-peer lending, REITs, or affiliate marketing, there are countless opportunities to earn passive income and achieve your financial goals. Take proactive steps to explore and pursue passive income opportunities today and set yourself on the path to financial independence and prosperity.

Creating Residual Income Streams
Individuals are increasingly seeking ways to build financial security and achieve greater freedom in their lives. One powerful strategy for achieving these goals is by creating residual income streams. Residual income, also known as passive income,

refers to the income generated from assets or activities that require minimal ongoing effort to maintain. Unlike active income, which requires continuous time and effort to earn, residual income allows individuals to generate revenue even when they're not actively working.

Residual income is derived from assets or activities that continue to generate income over time with minimal ongoing effort or active involvement. These income streams can come from a variety of sources, including rental properties, dividend-paying stocks, interest-bearing investments, royalties, licensing agreements, online businesses, and more. The key characteristic of residual income is that it continues to generate revenue even when you're not actively working, providing a source of passive cash flow that can contribute to your financial well-being.

Residual income offers a range of benefits that can significantly enhance your financial situation and quality of life. Perhaps the most attractive aspect of residual income is the passive cash flow it generates. Unlike active income, which requires continuous time and effort to earn, residual income allows you to earn money while you sleep. Whether it's rental income from properties, dividends from stocks, or royalties from creative works, residual income provides a steady stream of cash flow that can support your financial needs and goals.It has the potential to scale and grow over time, increasing your earning potential and building long-term wealth. With the right strategies and investments, you can leverage residual income to achieve your financial goals, whether it's saving for retirement, paying off debt, or pursuing your dreams. Residual income provides a pathway to financial independence and allows you to create the lifestyle you desire and it often comes with tax advantages that can further enhance your financial situation. Many passive income sources, such as rental properties and dividends, are taxed at lower rates than ordinary income. Additionally, certain investments and business activities may qualify for tax deductions or credits, reducing your overall tax liability and increasing your after-tax income.

Now that we've explored the concept and benefits of residual income, let's discuss practical strategies for creating residual income streams.One of the most popular ways to generate residual income is by investing in rental properties. By purchasing residential or commercial real estate and renting it out to tenants, you can earn passive rental income on a monthly basis. Rental properties offer the potential for steady cash flow, long-term appreciation, and tax benefits such as depreciation deductions.Investing in dividend-paying stocks, bonds, mutual funds, and other securities can provide passive income in the form of dividends, interest, and capital gains. By building a diversified investment portfolio, you can generate passive income while benefiting from the growth of the financial markets. Consider working with a financial advisor to develop an investment strategy that aligns with your goals and risk tolerance.

If you enjoy writing, blogging can be a lucrative way to generate passive income. By creating valuable content and attracting a loyal audience, you can monetize your blog through advertising, affiliate marketing, sponsored content, and digital products. With dedication and persistence, a successful blog can generate passive income for years to come.If you have creative works or intellectual property, consider licensing them to third parties for use in exchange for royalties. This could include licensing your music, artwork, photographs, books, software, or inventions to companies or individuals for commercial use. Licensing agreements allow you to earn passive income from your intellectual property while retaining ownership and control.

 Creating residual income streams is a powerful strategy for building wealth, achieving financial independence, and enjoying greater freedom in your life. Whether it's through rental properties, dividend-paying stocks, digital products, affiliate marketing, or other passive income opportunities, there are countless ways to generate passive income and achieve your financial goals. By diversifying your income sources and leveraging passive income streams, you can create a more stable and secure financial future for yourself and your loved ones. Take action today to start building residual income streams and unlock the potential for long-term wealth and prosperity.

Cultivate Discipline and Patience

Delayed Gratification: The Key to Success

We live in a society that values instant gratification, where we can access information, goods, and services with the click of a button. However, the ability to delay gratification is a crucial skill that can significantly impact our success and well-being in various aspects of life.

Delayed gratification refers to the ability to resist the temptation of immediate rewards or pleasures in favor of larger, more significant rewards that are obtained after a period of waiting, effort, or self-control. It involves sacrificing short-term pleasure or satisfaction for the sake of achieving long-term goals, aspirations, or outcomes. The concept was popularized in the 1960s by psychologist Walter Mischel through his famous marshmallow experiment, which demonstrated the correlation between delayed gratification and success in various areas of life.It plays a pivotal role in shaping our behavior, decisions, and outcomes across multiple domains, including personal finance, education, career, health, relationships, and overall well-being. It strengthens our self-discipline and willpower, enabling us to resist temptations and distractions that may derail us from our goals. It empowers us to make conscious, intentional choices that align with our values and it promotes more thoughtful, deliberate decision-making by encouraging us to consider the long-term consequences and benefits of our actions. It helps us weigh the trade-offs between immediate rewards and future outcomes. Instead of giving in to immediate gratification or giving up when faced with obstacles, we develop the resilience and determination to persevere and overcome obstacles on the path to success. leading to wiser choices and better outcomes.

   While delayed gratification may not come naturally to everyone, it is a skill that can be cultivated and strengthened with practice. Establish clear, specific, and achievable goals that align with your values, aspirations, and priorities. Break down large goals into smaller, manageable steps or milestones, and create a plan of action to work towards them systematically and Cultivate self-awareness by reflecting on your thoughts, feelings, and behaviors related to gratification and impulse control. Identify situations or triggers that tempt you to seek immediate rewards and explore alternative coping strategies or responses. Use implementation intentions or if-then planning to pre-commit to specific actions or behaviors in response to anticipated challenges or temptations. For example, if faced with the temptation to indulge in impulse spending, you might say, "If I feel the urge to make an impulse purchase, then I will wait 24 hours before making a decision."

Engage in structured exercises or activities that require you to delay gratification and exercise self-control. For example, the classic marshmallow test involves resisting the immediate temptation to eat a marshmallow in exchange for receiving two marshmallows later. Other exercises may involve delaying consumption of a favorite treat, delaying access to digital devices, or delaying gratification in social situations and trying to Develop patience and persistence by embracing the journey of growth and self-improvement. Understand that achieving meaningful goals and outcomes often requires time, effort, and perseverance. Stay focused on the long-term benefits and keep moving forward, even in the face of obstacles or setbacks.

Delayed gratification is a powerful mindset and skill that can profoundly impact our success, happiness, and well-being in life. By prioritizing long-term goals over short-term pleasures, we can cultivate self-discipline, make wiser decisions, and achieve greater fulfillment and success in various aspects of life. Whether it's pursuing academic or career goals, managing finances, maintaining healthy habits, or building strong relationships, practicing delayed gratification empowers us to live more purposefully and achieve our full potential. Embrace the journey of delayed gratification, and unlock the keys to success, resilience, and fulfillment in life.

Staying Focused on Long-Term Goals

In the pursuit of our dreams and aspirations, it's easy to get sidetracked by distractions, setbacks, and the allure of short-term gratification. However, the ability to stay focused on long-term goals is a critical skill that can determine our success, fulfillment, and overall quality of life. In this comprehensive guide, we'll explore the importance of staying focused on long-term goals, the challenges we face in maintaining focus, and practical strategies for cultivating and sustaining our commitment to achieving our most significant aspirations.

Long-term goals are the visions, dreams, and aspirations that we set for ourselves over an extended period, typically spanning months, years, or even decades. These goals represent the outcomes we desire to achieve in various areas of our lives, such as career, education, finances, health, relationships, personal growth, and contribution to society. Long-term goals provide direction, purpose, and motivation, guiding our actions and decisions as we navigate through life's journey.Staying focused on long-term goals is essential for several reasons.

Long-term goals provide clarity of purpose and direction, helping us prioritize our time, energy, and resources towards what truly matters to us. By staying focused on our long-term vision, we can align our actions with our values and aspirations, leading to a more meaningful and purposeful life and it serves as powerful sources of motivation and inspiration, driving us to overcome obstacles, persevere through challenges, and persist in the face of setbacks. When we remain focused on our long-term aspirations, we are more likely to stay committed and resilient in pursuing our dreams, even when the journey becomes difficult or uncertain.staying focused on long-term goals provide a framework for making informed decisions and choices that are aligned with our desired outcomes. When faced with competing priorities or opportunities, staying focused on our long-term vision helps us evaluate options, weigh trade-offs, and make decisions that move us closer to our goals.

Despite the importance of staying focused on long-term goals, many individuals encounter challenges that hinder their ability to maintain focus and commitment. The allure of immediate rewards or pleasures can distract us from our long-term goals, leading to impulsive actions and decisions that undermine our progress. Temptations such as procrastination, indulgence, or instant gratification can derail our focus and pull us away from our desired outcomes.The pursuit of long-term goals often requires sustained effort, persistence, and resilience over an extended period. However, excessive stress, overwhelm, and burnout can drain our energy and motivation, making it challenging to stay focused and committed to our goals amidst competing demands and pressures.one of the factors that hinder us the most is fear of failure or success. It paralyzes us with doubt, insecurity, and self-sabotage, preventing us from taking action towards our long-term goals. Negative beliefs, self-limiting beliefs, and perfectionism can undermine our confidence and deter us from pursuing our dreams with conviction and determination.

Despite the challenges we face, there are practical strategies we can employ to stay focused on our long-term goals and maximize our chances of success.Take time to clarify your long-term goals, aspirations, and vision for the future. Identify what truly matters to you, what you want to achieve, and why it's important to you. Write down your goals in specific, measurable, achievable, relevant, and time-bound (SMART) format to create a clear roadmap for success and you need to Break down your long-term goals into smaller, manageable steps or milestones that you can work towards incrementally. Focus on making progress one step at a time, celebrating small victories along the way, and staying committed to the process of growth and development.Prioritize your time, energy, and resources towards activities and tasks that align with your long-term goals and values. Identify your most important priorities and eliminate or delegate non-essential tasks that detract from your focus and productivity. Create daily, weekly, and monthly plans to stay organized and on track towards your goals and Cultivate self-discipline and positive habits that support your long-term goals and aspirations. Practice consistency, persistence, and resilience in pursuing your goals, even when faced with challenges or setbacks. Establish daily routines, rituals, and rituals that reinforce your commitment to success and help you stay focused on your goals.

And let me conclude it by saying,staying focused on long-term goals is a transformative journey that requires dedication, discipline, and resilience. By clarifying your vision, prioritizing your time and energy, managing distractions, cultivating positive habits, and seeking support from others, you can stay committed to achieving your most significant aspirations and create a life of purpose, fulfillment, and success. Embrace the challenges, celebrate the victories, and stay focused on the journey of growth and transformation as you pursue your long-term goals with passion and perseverance.

Overcoming Challenges and Setbacks

Life is filled with ups and downs, successes and failures, triumphs and setbacks. While facing challenges and setbacks is an inevitable part of the human experience, how we respond to adversity can profoundly impact our personal growth, resilience, and overall well-being.we'll explore the nature of challenges and setbacks, their common sources, and practical strategies for overcoming them with resilience, perseverance, and grace. Challenges and setbacks are obstacles, difficulties, or adverse circumstances that impede our progress, hinder our success, or disrupt our plans and aspirations. They can manifest in various forms, such as personal struggles, professional setbacks, relationship conflicts, health issues, financial problems, or external circumstances beyond our control. Challenges and setbacks are a natural part of life's journey and provide opportunities for learning, growth, and self-discovery.

Challenges and setbacks can arise from a multitude of sources. Internal factors such as self-doubt, fear, limiting beliefs, perfectionism, and lack of confidence can create barriers to success and resilience. Negative thought patterns, self-sabotaging behaviors, and low self-esteem can undermine our ability to overcome challenges and setbacks effectively. External circumstances such as economic downturns, natural disasters, political instability, global pandemics, or unforeseen events beyond our control can create challenges and setbacks in various areas of our lives. These external factors can disrupt our plans, routines, and expectations, leading to stress, uncertainty, and adversity.

Health-related challenges such as illness, injury, chronic pain, mental health issues, or disabilities can pose significant obstacles to our physical, emotional, and psychological well-being. Managing health challenges and setbacks requires resilience, self-care, and support from healthcare professionals, loved ones, and community resources.

While facing challenges and setbacks can be daunting, there are practical strategies we can employ to navigate through adversity and emerge stronger, wiser, and more resilient.

Resilience is the ability to bounce back from adversity, adapt to change, and thrive in the face of challenges. Cultivate resilience by developing coping skills, positive thinking patterns, and emotional regulation strategies. Practice self-care, mindfulness, and self-compassion to nurture your well-being and build inner strength.Shift your perspective on challenges and setbacks by reframing them as opportunities for growth, learning, and self-discovery. Embrace adversity as a natural part of life's journey and a catalyst for personal transformation. Look for the lessons, silver linings, and hidden blessings in every challenge you encounter.Cultivate a growth mindset that embraces challenges, failures, and setbacks as opportunities for learning and growth. View setbacks as temporary setbacks rather than permanent failures, and focus on the lessons and insights gained from each experience. Believe in your ability to learn, adapt, and overcome obstacles on the path to success and Be kind and compassionate towards yourself when facing challenges and setbacks. Treat yourself with the same care, understanding, and empathy that you would offer to a friend or loved one in a similar situation. Practice self-compassion by acknowledging your efforts, validating your emotions, and practicing self-care.

Facing challenges and setbacks is an inevitable part of life's journey, but it's how we respond to adversity that ultimately defines our character, resilience, and success. By cultivating resilience, reframing challenges as opportunities, setting realistic expectations, practicing problem-solving skills, building a support network, practicing self-compassion, maintaining a growth mindset, and seeking professional help when needed, we can overcome challenges and setbacks with grace and resilience. Embrace the journey of growth, and trust in your ability to navigate through adversity with courage, strength, and resilience.

Network and Surround Yourself with Success

Importance of Networking

In today's interconnected world, networking has become a fundamental aspect of professional and personal success. Whether you're seeking new career opportunities, expanding your business, or simply looking to build meaningful relationships, networking plays a crucial role in opening doors, creating opportunities, and fostering growth.Networking refers to the process of building and nurturing relationships with others for mutual benefit. It involves connecting with individuals, organizations, or communities to exchange information, ideas, resources, and support. Networking can take place in various settings, including professional events, social gatherings, online platforms, and industry conferences. Whether it's making new contacts, strengthening existing relationships, or expanding your network, networking is a proactive and strategic approach to building connections and fostering opportunities for collaboration and growth.

Networking is essential for several reasons.It provides access to a wide range of career opportunities, including job openings, internships, mentorship programs, and professional development opportunities. By expanding your network, you can tap into hidden job markets, gain insights into industry trends, and connect with influential leaders and decision-makers who can support your career advancement.For entrepreneurs, small business owners, and freelancers, networking is vital for building and growing their ventures. By networking with potential clients, partners, investors, and collaborators, you can generate leads, attract new customers, and explore strategic partnerships that can fuel business growth and expansion.It provides access to a wealth of resources, including information, tools, funding, and support networks. Whether it's seeking advice, recommendations, or referrals, your network can serve as a valuable source of guidance and assistance in navigating challenges, seizing opportunities, and overcoming obstacles on your journey to success.

Networking offers numerous benefits that can significantly impact your personal and professional life.Networking opens doors to new opportunities, connections, and collaborations that may not be accessible through traditional channels. Whether it's finding a new job, securing a business partnership, or discovering a mentor, networking increases your visibility and exposure to opportunities in your field or industry.By actively engaging in networking activities, you can increase your visibility and establish yourself as a credible and respected professional in your field. Attending industry events, participating in online communities, and sharing valuable insights can help you build your reputation and position yourself as a thought leader in your industry.Networking provides opportunities for continuous learning and professional development. By interacting with individuals who possess diverse backgrounds, experiences, and perspectives, you can broaden your knowledge, acquire new skills, and stay abreast of industry trends and innovations.It encourages you to step out of your comfort zone, meet new people, and develop interpersonal skills that can enhance your confidence and self-esteem. By building relationships with others and engaging in meaningful conversations, you can boost your social skills, communication abilities, and overall confidence in social and professional settings.

To maximize the benefits of networking, consider implementing the following strategies:

1.Define your networking goals and objectives, whether it's expanding your professional contacts, finding a new job, or growing your business. Clarify what you hope to achieve through networking and develop a plan to guide your efforts.

2.Approach networking with authenticity, sincerity, and a genuine interest in building meaningful connections. Focus on building rapport, listening actively, and showing empathy towards others. Avoid being overly transactional or self-promotional, and prioritize building relationships based on trust and mutual respect.

3.Utilize online networking platforms such as LinkedIn, Twitter, and professional networking groups to connect with professionals in your field. Participate in group discussions, share valuable content, and engage with others in your industry to build your online presence and expand your network.

4.Look for opportunities to add value and support to your network by sharing insights, resources, and opportunities that may benefit others. Offer assistance, advice, or introductions whenever possible, and be generous with your time and expertise.

5.Invest time and effort in nurturing and maintaining relationships with your network contacts. Stay in touch regularly through emails, phone calls, coffee meetings, or social gatherings. Show genuine interest in their goals, achievements, and challenges, and offer support and encouragement when needed.

6.Follow up with new contacts promptly after networking events to express gratitude and reinforce the connection. Follow through on any commitments or promises you've made, whether it's sending a follow-up email, making an introduction, or providing information or assistance.

Networking is a powerful tool for building connections, creating opportunities, and fostering growth and success in both your personal and professional life. By actively engaging in networking activities, you can expand your professional network, enhance your visibility and credibility, and access valuable resources and support networks. Whether it's attending networking events, leveraging online platforms, or cultivating relationships with others, networking offers numerous benefits that can propel you towards your goals and aspirations. Embrace networking as a strategic and proactive approach to building connections and advancing your career or business, and watch as it opens doors to new opportunities and possibilities for growth and success.

Mentors and Role Models

In the journey of life, having mentors and role models can make a profound difference in our personal and professional development. Mentors are experienced individuals who offer guidance, support, and wisdom based on their own knowledge and expertise, while role models are individuals we admire and aspire to emulate. In this comprehensive guide, we'll explore the importance of mentors and role models, their impact on our lives, and practical strategies for finding, cultivating, and benefiting from these valuable relationships.

Mentors and role models play distinct but complementary roles in our lives. Mentors are individuals who possess knowledge, skills, and experience in a particular field or domain and are willing to share their insights and expertise with others. They serve as trusted advisors, coaches, and guides, offering valuable feedback, advice, and support to help their mentees navigate challenges, seize opportunities, and achieve their goals. Mentors often provide mentorship through formal or informal relationships, coaching sessions, or structured programs aimed at fostering professional growth and development.

Role models are individuals whom we admire, respect, and look up to for their qualities, achievements, and values. They serve as inspirational figures who embody the traits, behaviors, and attitudes we aspire to emulate in our own lives. Role models can be found in various domains, including sports, entertainment, business, academia, politics, and community leadership. Whether it's their integrity, resilience, leadership, or innovation, role models inspire us to strive for excellence and pursue our dreams with passion and purpose.

Mentors and role models play a crucial role in shaping our personal and professional development for several reasons:

1.Mentors provide invaluable guidance, support, and advice based on their own experiences and insights. They offer practical wisdom, perspective, and encouragement to help their mentees navigate challenges, overcome obstacles, and make informed decisions in their personal and professional lives. Role models inspire us through their actions, achievements, and example, showing us what is possible and motivating us to reach for greater heights.

2.Mentors possess specialized knowledge, skills, and expertise in their respective fields, which they generously share with their mentees. They offer insights, strategies, and best practices gleaned from their own experiences, helping mentees accelerate their learning and development and avoid common pitfalls and mistakes. Role models demonstrate excellence in their chosen fields, serving as benchmarks of achievement and sources of inspiration for others to follow.

3.Mentors and role models often have extensive networks and connections within their industries or communities, which they can leverage to benefit their mentees and followers. They provide introductions, referrals, and networking opportunities that can open doors to new relationships, collaborations, and career opportunities. By associating with mentors and role models, individuals can expand their professional networks, gain visibility, and access valuable resources and support networks.

4.Mentors and role models contribute to our personal growth and development by challenging us to stretch beyond our comfort zones, expand our horizons, and pursue ambitious goals. They provide constructive feedback, encouragement, and accountability, pushing us to strive for continuous improvement and excellence in our endeavors. Through their mentorship and example, individuals can cultivate essential skills such as resilience, adaptability, and emotional intelligence, which are critical for success in today's rapidly changing world.

5.Perhaps most importantly, mentors and role models inspire and motivate us to dream big, set ambitious goals, and pursue our passions with

dedication and perseverance. Their stories of triumph over adversity, resilience in the face of challenges, and unwavering commitment to their ideals fuel our own aspirations and ignite our inner drive to achieve greatness. By witnessing the achievements and successes of mentors and role models, individuals gain confidence, belief in themselves, and a sense of purpose that propels them forward on their own journey to success.
Finding and cultivating mentors and role models requires proactive effort and intentionality:

1.Clarify your goals, aspirations, and areas where you could benefit from guidance and support. Consider what qualities, skills, or achievements you admire in others and seek mentors and role models who embody those traits.

2.Actively seek out opportunities to expand your network and connect with individuals who can serve as mentors or role models. Attend industry events, networking functions, and professional conferences where you can meet experienced professionals and leaders in your field.

3.Even if you don't have direct access to a particular role model, you can still learn from their example and apply their principles and strategies to your own life. Study their biographies, speeches, interviews, or writings to glean insights into their mindset, approach, and key success factors.

4. Don't be afraid to reach out to individuals you admire and respect to inquire about mentorship opportunities. Be respectful, genuine, and specific in your request, explaining why you admire their work and how you believe their guidance could benefit your personal or professional development.

5. As you benefit from the guidance and support of mentors and role models, consider paying it forward by mentoring others and serving as a role model for those who are just starting out on their journey. By sharing your knowledge, experience, and wisdom with others, you can create a ripple effect of positive impact and contribute to the growth and success of future generations.

In conclusion Mentors and role models are invaluable sources of guidance, inspiration, and support on the journey to success and growth. Whether through formal mentorship relationships, informal connections, or admiration from afar, mentors and role models play a critical role in shaping our personal and professional development, helping us navigate challenges, seize opportunities, and achieve our goals and aspirations. By actively seeking out mentors and role models who embody the qualities and values we admire, and by cultivating authentic relationships based on trust, respect, and mutual benefit, we can accelerate our learning, expand our horizons, and realize our fullest potential. Embrace the guidance and inspiration of mentors and role models, and let their wisdom and example illuminate your path to success and fulfillment.

Joining Mastermind Groups and Communities

In today's interconnected world, joining mastermind groups and communities has emerged as a powerful strategy for personal and professional growth. These collaborative networks bring together like-minded individuals who share common goals, interests, or challenges, providing a platform for learning, collaboration, and support. In this comprehensive guide, we'll explore the benefits of joining mastermind groups and communities, how they work, and practical strategies for finding and participating in these transformative networks.

Mastermind groups and communities are collaborative networks of individuals who come together to share knowledge, expertise, and resources to support each other's growth and success. These groups typically consist of a small number of members who meet regularly, either in person or virtually, to discuss their goals, challenges, and ideas, and to provide feedback, accountability, and encouragement to one another.The concept of mastermind groups was popularized by Napoleon Hill in his book "Think and Grow Rich," where he described the power of collective brainstorming and collaboration in achieving success. Since then, mastermind groups and communities have evolved into diverse networks spanning various industries, professions, interests, and goals.

Joining mastermind groups and communities offers numerous benefits for personal and professional growth.Mastermind groups and communities bring together individuals with diverse backgrounds, experiences, and perspectives, providing access to a wealth of knowledge, expertise, and insights. By tapping into the collective wisdom of the group, members can gain new perspectives, learn from others' experiences, and access solutions to their challenges more effectively than they could on their own and offer valuable networking opportunities, allowing members to connect with like-minded individuals, expand their professional networks, and forge meaningful relationships. These connections can lead to collaborations, partnerships, and new opportunities for growth, such as joint ventures, referrals, or shared resources.

To find and participate in mastermind groups and communities effectively, consider the following strategies:

1.Clarify your goals, interests, and areas where you could benefit from support, feedback, or collaboration. Determine what you hope to achieve by joining a mastermind group or community and what specific topics or themes are most relevant to your objectives.

2.Explore online platforms, social media groups, professional organizations, and community forums to find mastermind groups and communities that align with your goals and interests. Look for groups that have active membership, relevant content, and positive reviews or recommendations from other members.

3.Before committing to joining a mastermind group or community, take the time to evaluate its fit and compatibility with your goals, values, and preferences. Consider factors such as group size, frequency of meetings, format, structure, and membership demographics to ensure that it aligns with your needs and expectations.

4.Once you've joined a mastermind group or community, make an effort to actively participate, engage with other members, and contribute to discussions and activities. Share your insights, experiences, and resources generously, and offer support and encouragement to fellow members as they pursue their goals.

In conclusion Joining mastermind groups and communities offers a valuable opportunity to tap into the collective wisdom, support, and resources of like-minded individuals who share common goals, interests, or challenges. Whether it's personal growth, professional development, or mutual support, mastermind groups and communities provide a supportive environment where members can learn from each other, collaborate on projects, and hold each other accountable for achieving their goals. By actively participating in mastermind groups and communities that align with your interests and aspirations, you can accelerate your growth, expand your network, and achieve greater success and fulfillment in all areas of your life. Embrace the power of collective wisdom and support, and let mastermind groups and communities be your guiding lights on the path to success and growth.

Giving Back and Philanthropy

The Power of Giving

At its core, giving is a universal act of kindness, compassion, and generosity that transcends cultural, social, and geographical boundaries. From small acts of kindness to large-scale philanthropy, giving has the power to transform lives, strengthen communities, and create positive change on a global scale. Giving encompasses a wide range of actions, from donating money to charitable organizations to volunteering time and expertise to support causes we care about.

Donating money to charitable organizations, nonprofits, or individuals in need to support their missions, programs, or initiatives or contributing time, skills, and expertise to support community projects, events, or initiatives aimed at addressing social, environmental, or humanitarian issues.Performing spontaneous acts of kindness, such as helping a stranger in need, paying for someone's meal, or offering words of encouragement and support.

Giving holds immense power to create positive change and impact lives in profound ways:

1. Giving provides essential resources, support, and assistance to individuals and communities facing poverty, hunger, homelessness, and other forms of hardship. By addressing immediate needs and providing long-term solutions, giving can help alleviate suffering and improve quality of life for those in need.

2. Giving empowers individuals to overcome challenges, achieve their potential, and lead fulfilling lives with dignity and self-respect. Whether through education, job training, or access to basic necessities, giving provides opportunities for people to build a better future for themselves and their families.

3. Giving fosters a sense of connection, belonging, and solidarity within communities by encouraging collaboration, cooperation, and mutual support among members. By working together to address common challenges and pursue shared goals, communities can become more resilient, inclusive, and vibrant.

In addition to its positive impact on others, giving offers numerous benefits for individuals who engage in acts of kindness and generosity:

1. Research has shown that giving can boost feelings of happiness, satisfaction, and overall well-

being. The act of giving triggers the release of neurotransmitters such as dopamine and endorphins, which are associated with feelings of pleasure and reward, leading to a "helper's high" that can elevate mood and reduce stress.

2.Giving fosters social connections and strengthens relationships with others by creating opportunities for meaningful interactions, shared experiences, and mutual support. By participating in giving activities, individuals can forge deeper bonds with friends, family members, and community members, leading to greater feelings of belonging and connection.

3.Engaging in acts of giving promotes personal growth and development by encouraging individuals to step outside of their comfort zones, challenge their assumptions, and develop new skills and perspectives. By volunteering, donating, or supporting causes they care about, individuals can expand their horizons, broaden their worldview, and cultivate qualities such as empathy, compassion, and resilience.

The power of giving is undeniable, touching hearts, changing lives, and creating a better world for all. Whether through financial donations, volunteerism, or acts of kindness and compassion, giving has the power to transform individuals, strengthen communities, and foster positive change on a global scale. By incorporating giving into our lives and embracing the values of kindness, empathy, and generosity, we can create a more compassionate, equitable, and inclusive world where everyone has the opportunity to thrive and succeed. Together, let's harness the power of giving to build a brighter future for generations to come.

Incorporating Philanthropy into Your Financial Plan

Philanthropy, the act of donating time, money, or resources to support charitable causes and initiatives, has the power to create positive change and make a lasting impact on individuals, communities, and society as a whole. By incorporating philanthropy into your financial plan, you can align your values with your financial goals, maximize your impact, and leave a legacy of generosity and compassion.Philanthropy encompasses a wide range of charitable activities and initiatives aimed at addressing social, environmental, and humanitarian issues.Establishing charitable trusts, endowments, or foundations to support causes you care about and leave a lasting impact on future generations.Making investments in businesses, projects, or initiatives that generate positive social or environmental outcomes in addition to financial returns.

Strategies for Incorporating Philanthropy into Your Financial Plan:

1. Start by defining your philanthropic mission and values, identifying the causes, issues, or initiatives that are most meaningful to you. Consider your passions, interests, and personal experiences, and think about how you can leverage your resources to make a meaningful impact in these areas.

2. Allocate a portion of your income or assets to support your philanthropic goals, and create a budget that reflects your giving priorities. Consider how much you can afford to give each year, and allocate your resources strategically to maximize their impact and effectiveness.

3. Before making charitable contributions, research organizations, nonprofits, or causes to ensure they align with your values and priorities. Evaluate their mission, impact, financial transparency, and effectiveness, and look for opportunities to support organizations that demonstrate accountability and good stewardship of resources.

4. Explore different giving vehicles and strategies that align with your philanthropic goals and financial situation. Consider options such as donor-advised funds, charitable trusts, endowments, or direct

donations to maximize tax benefits, flexibility, and long-term impact.

5. Regularly evaluate and measure the impact of your philanthropic efforts to ensure they are achieving their intended outcomes. Monitor progress, track results, and adjust your giving strategy as needed to maximize effectiveness and address emerging needs or opportunities.

Incorporating philanthropy into your financial plan is a powerful way to align your financial goals with your personal values and priorities, maximize your impact, and leave a lasting legacy of generosity and compassion. By defining your philanthropic mission and values, setting specific goals and priorities, and strategically allocating your resources, you can make a meaningful difference in the lives of individuals and communities while enriching your own life with meaning, fulfillment, and purpose. Embrace the power of philanthropy to create positive change and leave a lasting impact that extends far beyond your lifetime.

Leaving a Legacy

Leaving a legacy is about more than just passing on material wealth; it's about creating a lasting impact that extends far beyond our own lives. Whether through our actions, values, achievements, or contributions, each of us has the opportunity to leave a legacy that shapes the world and inspires future generations.Legacy is the imprint we leave on the world through our actions, words, and deeds. It encompasses the impact we have on others, the values we instill in future generations, and the contributions we make to society. While legacy is often associated with material wealth or inheritance, it goes beyond financial assets to encompass intangible qualities such as character, wisdom, and influence.Leaving a legacy is a deeply personal and individual journey, shaped by our values, beliefs, and experiences. It's about living a life of purpose and meaning, making choices that align with our core principles, and leaving behind a positive and lasting impact on the world.

Leaving a legacy gives our lives meaning and purpose, providing a sense of fulfillment and satisfaction that comes from knowing we've made a difference in the world. By living according to our values and principles, we can create a legacy that reflects our deepest aspirations and beliefs.It gives us the opportunity to make a positive impact on the world and leave it a better place than we found it. Whether through acts of kindness, charitable giving, or social advocacy, we can contribute to meaningful change and leave a lasting legacy of compassion, generosity, and service and serve as a source of inspiration and guidance for future generations, showing them what is possible and inspiring them to follow in our footsteps. Whether through our achievements, values, or contributions, we can leave behind a legacy that motivates others to strive for greatness and pursue their dreams.

Here are some practical strategies for leaving a meaningful legacy:

1.Start by defining your core values, principles, and beliefs. Consider what matters most to you and what you want to be remembered for. Your values will serve as the foundation for your legacy and guide your actions and decisions throughout your life.

2.Live your life with intention and purpose, making choices that align with your values and aspirations. Consider how your actions and decisions today will impact your legacy tomorrow, and strive to leave behind a positive and meaningful imprint on the world.

3.Give back to your community and society by supporting causes and initiatives that align with your values and priorities. Whether through volunteerism, charitable giving, or advocacy, make a positive impact on the world and leave behind a legacy of generosity, compassion, and social responsibility.

4.Be mindful of your environmental impact and take steps to reduce your carbon footprint and preserve natural resources for future generations. Embrace sustainability practices in your daily life and support initiatives that promote environmental conservation and stewardship.

5.Document your life story, experiences, and wisdom to pass on to future generations. Write memoirs, record oral histories, or create legacy projects that capture your unique journey and insights, ensuring that your legacy lives on for years to come.

Leaving a legacy is a profound and deeply personal journey that reflects our values, passions, and aspirations. By living with intention and purpose, cultivating meaningful relationships, and making a positive impact on the world, each of us has the power to leave behind a legacy that inspires, empowers, and uplifts future generations. Whether through our actions, values, or contributions, let us strive to leave a lasting imprint on the world that reflects the best of who we are and what we stand for. Embrace the opportunity to leave a meaningful legacy, and let your life be a beacon of hope, inspiration, and possibility for generations to come.

Conclusion

Recap of Key Strategies

Throughout this guide, we've explored a wide range of strategies aimed at achieving success, personal growth, and fulfillment in various aspects of life. From financial planning and career development to personal well-being and social impact, each strategy offers valuable insights and practical tips for navigating the complexities of modern life. In this recap, we'll review some of the key strategies covered in this guide and highlight their importance in shaping our journey towards success and happiness.One of the fundamental pillars of success is sound financial planning and wealth management. By setting clear financial goals, budgeting effectively, and investing wisely, individuals can secure their financial future and create opportunities for growth and prosperity.

Establish a budget that reflects your income, expenses, and savings goals, and track your spending to ensure financial discipline and accountability and develop a diversified investment portfolio tailored to your risk tolerance, time horizon, and financial objectives, and regularly review and adjust your investment strategy as needed.Integrate philanthropy into your financial plan by allocating resources to support charitable causes and initiatives that reflect your values and priorities.

Career development and professional growth are essential for achieving success and fulfillment in the workplace. By honing your skills, cultivating a growth mindset, and building a strong professional network, you can unlock new opportunities and advance your career. Key strategies in this area include:
1.Invest in ongoing learning and skill development to stay competitive in your field and adapt to evolving trends and technologies.
2.Cultivate relationships with peers, mentors, and industry leaders to expand your professional network, gain valuable insights, and access new opportunities.
3.Define clear career goals and create a roadmap for achieving them, including short-term milestones and action plans to keep you on track.

Personal well-being and self-care are essential for maintaining balance, resilience, and overall happiness in life. By prioritizing self-care, managing stress effectively, and cultivating positive habits, individuals can enhance their physical, mental, and emotional well-being.Make self-care a priority by engaging in activities that promote relaxation, rejuvenation, and self-reflection, such as exercise, meditation, and hobbies and develop coping mechanisms and stress management techniques to deal with life's challenges effectively and maintain a sense of calm and perspective.

Making a positive impact in the community and society at large is a fulfilling way to contribute to the greater good and leave a lasting legacy. By volunteering, advocating for social causes, and supporting organizations that address pressing issues, individuals can create meaningful change and inspire others to do the same.

Key strategies in this area include:

1. Donate your time, skills, and expertise to support local charities, nonprofits, or community organizations that address issues you care about.
2. Adopt environmentally sustainable practices in your daily life and support businesses, organizations, and initiatives that prioritize sustainability and environmental conservation.

Success is a multifaceted journey that encompasses various aspects of life, including financial stability, career advancement, personal well-being, and social impact. By adopting key strategies in each of these areas, individuals can navigate the complexities of modern life more effectively and achieve greater success, happiness, and fulfillment. Whether it's setting SMART financial goals, advancing your career through continuous learning and mentorship, prioritizing self-care and well-being, or making a positive impact in the community, each strategy plays a vital role in shaping our journey towards a more purposeful and meaningful life. As you embark on your own path to success, remember to reflect on these key strategies and incorporate them into your daily life to unlock your full potential and create a lasting impact in the world.

Taking Action on Your Path to Millionaire Success

Becoming a millionaire is a goal that many aspire to achieve, but few actually attain. While it may seem like an insurmountable challenge, the truth is that with the right mindset, strategies, and actions, anyone can reach millionaire status. In this comprehensive guide, we'll explore the key steps you can take to turn your dreams of millionaire success into reality. From setting clear goals and cultivating a wealthy mindset to taking decisive action and overcoming obstacles, we'll cover everything you need to know to embark on your journey to financial abundance.

The first step on your path to millionaire success is to set clear, achievable goals and create a compelling vision for your future. Without a clear sense of direction and purpose, it's easy to get lost or discouraged along the way.Take the time to define what success means to you personally. Is it achieving a specific financial milestone, attaining a certain level of freedom and flexibility, or making a positive impact in the world? Clarifying your definition of success will help you set goals that align with your values and priorities and create specific, measurable, achievable, relevant, and time-bound (SMART) goals that will guide your journey to millionaire success. Break down your goals into smaller, actionable steps, and track your progress regularly to stay on course and use visualization techniques to imagine yourself achieving your goals and living the life of your dreams. Picture yourself enjoying the benefits of financial abundance, whether it's traveling the world, starting a business, or supporting causes you care about.

Achieving millionaire success requires more than just setting goals; it also requires cultivating a wealth mindset that empowers you to think and act like a millionaire.Shift your mindset from scarcity to abundance by focusing on opportunities rather than limitations. Believe that there is more than enough wealth and abundance to go around, and that you have the power to create unlimited opportunities for yourself and develop positive money habits such as saving regularly, investing wisely, and living within your means. Practice delayed gratification and

prioritize long-term financial security over short-term pleasures.
Identify and challenge any limiting beliefs you may have about money, success, or your ability to achieve your goals. Replace negative thoughts and self-doubt with positive affirmations and empowering beliefs that reinforce your confidence and determination.

Once you've set clear goals and developed a wealth mindset, the next step is to take decisive action towards achieving your objectives. Action is the key to turning your dreams into reality and moving closer to millionaire success. Here are some strategies to help you take decisive action and make progress towards your goals:

1. Develop positive money habits such as saving regularly, investing wisely, and living within your means. Practice delayed gratification and prioritize long-term financial security over short-term pleasures.

2. Identify and challenge any limiting beliefs you may have about money, success, or your ability to achieve your goals. Replace negative thoughts and self-doubt with positive affirmations and empowering beliefs that reinforce your confidence and determination.

Once you've set clear goals and developed a wealth mindset, the next step is to take decisive action towards achieving your objectives. Action is the key to turning your dreams into reality and moving closer to millionaire success.Break down your goals into smaller, manageable tasks and prioritize them based on their importance and urgency. Focus on taking consistent, incremental steps towards your goals each day, rather than trying to accomplish everything at once and develop a detailed plan of action that outlines the specific steps you need to take to achieve your goals. Set deadlines and milestones to keep yourself accountable and track your progress along the way.Success rarely happens overnight, so it's essential to stay persistent and resilient in the face of challenges and obstacles. Keep pushing forward, even when things get tough, and maintain a positive attitude and belief in your ability to succeed.

No journey to millionaire success is without its share of obstacles and challenges. From financial setbacks to personal doubts and fears, there will inevitably be roadblocks along the way. The key is to approach these challenges with resilience, determination, and a willingness to adapt.Cultivate strong problem-solving skills that will help you navigate obstacles and find creative solutions to challenges. Break down problems into manageable components and brainstorm potential solutions, seeking input and advice from trusted advisors when needed. Remain flexible and adaptive in your approach to achieving your goals, recognizing that circumstances may change along the way. Be open to adjusting your plans and strategies as needed to overcome obstacles and seize new opportunities and view failure as an opportunity for growth and learning rather than a setback. Analyze what went wrong, identify lessons learned, and use that knowledge to improve your approach and strategy moving forward.

As you progress on your journey to millionaire success, it's essential to take time to celebrate your achievements and acknowledge your progress along the way. Celebrating milestones not only boosts your morale and motivation but also reinforces your commitment to your goals. Here are some ways to celebrate your success and stay motivated on your path to millionaire success:

1. Take time to acknowledge and celebrate your achievements, no matter how small or insignificant they may seem. Recognize the effort and dedication you've put into pursuing your goals and congratulate yourself for your progress.

2. Treat yourself to rewards and incentives for reaching significant milestones and achieving key objectives. Whether it's a small indulgence like a

spa day or a weekend getaway, reward yourself for your hard work and perseverance.

3.Share your success with others and celebrate your achievements with friends, family, and loved ones. Share your progress on social media, host a celebration or gathering, or simply take time to reflect and express gratitude for how far you've come.

4.Once you've reached a milestone or achieved a significant goal, challenge yourself to set new goals and objectives that will continue to push you outside of your comfort zone and drive your progress forward. Keep striving for excellence and pursuing new opportunities for growth and success.

Becoming a millionaire is not an easy feat, but with the right mindset, strategies, and actions, it is entirely achievable. By setting clear goals, cultivating a wealth mindset, taking decisive action, and overcoming obstacles along the way, you can turn your dreams of millionaire success into reality. Remember that success is not just about reaching a destination; it's about embracing the journey and the lessons learned along the way. Stay focused, stay determined, and stay committed to your goals, and you'll soon find yourself on the path to millionaire success.

www.ingramcontent.com/pod-product-compliance
Lightning Source LLC
Chambersburg PA
CBHW070111230526
45472CB00004B/1221